BY ARLETTE THOMAS-FLETCHER

# DREAMER'S JOURNEY

## ILLUSTRATED BY KOTIRING

1

**Library of Congress Number: 1-11522920559**
**Printed in the United States of America**

# Dedication

To Joel and Charles, my wonderful sons, who I taught to enjoy running, playing, to use your imagination, and to dream out loud.

Never stop dreaming and working on your future. You are the inspiration for this book.

Special thank you to my friends at NYWIFT at the New Works Lab.

# On the road to your dreams

Jumping rope, flying kites and watching butterflies.

Daydreaming of happy thoughts.

Twirl in circles, play soccer, and dance around to your own music.

It's also fun to play hide-and-seek with friends.

There are no rules to dreaming!

# Did you know that animals dream, too?

# Create your dreams in many ways

Paint a work of art, cut and paste, or draw a beautiful picture.

# Dreaming is imagining wonderful things!

Paint a work of art, cut and paste, or draw a beautiful picture.

9

# You can anything you want to be

**A plumber**

**A building contractor**

**A bus driver**

Dreaming allows you to be free.

When you look at the sky, do you wonder how the birds fly?

Dreaming is just allowing your mind to wonder and think about beautiful things.

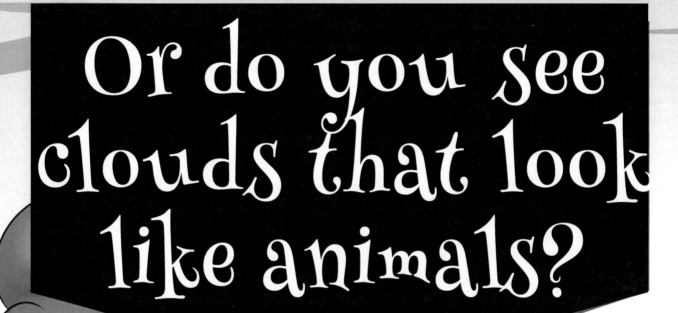

Or do you see clouds that look like animals?

What do you see in the clouds?

Your heart is where your dreams are stored Open it up and explore the many pieces of your dreams!

**A mechanic**

**An artist**

**A surgeon**

# Unleash your imagination

The sky is the limit!
You can be whatever you dream.

**An architect**

**A computer programmer**

**A hairdresser**

# Cut and paste a beautiful picture

# Think about fun things

Be a dreamer and picture what your future looks like. Do what you love to do!

# You can create your dreams with friends

17

# Take a journey - read a story

Books can take your imagination to a very special place in time.

# What things have you learned?

Tell what you have learned in pictures and drawings. You can talk about it with your Mom and Dad.

# Put on your thinking helmet!

Now, think about what you want to be. Make a wish (like when you blow out the candles on your birthday cake). Then, look at all the choices you must make your wish come true.

# You can be any-thing you want to be

A gamer

A doctor

A fire person

# There are so many choices to make

A singer

A chef

A dancer

# Read your dream-story aloud

You worked so hard.
You should be very proud.

# Let's draw pictures of what you like to do

# Draw a picture of your dream

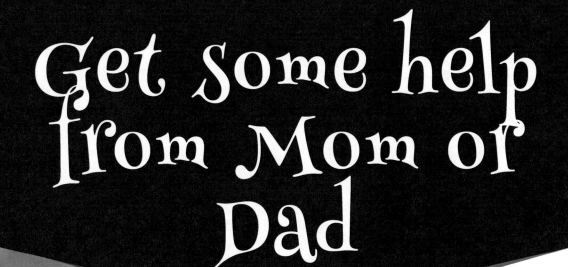

# Get some help from Mom or Dad

Sometimes it takes a team

# If you have a pet, let them join in your dream fun

Draw a picture of all you have done.

# Use all the space you need to create your dream

# Creating a dream is hard work

Don't rush to finish. Remember, it's your dream.

# You've almost finished your dreamer's journey

# Let's see what you drew

# Now, go to sleep. Dream BIG!!!

It's your future

Made in United States
North Haven, CT
22 September 2022

24443789R00020